C000096307

Chinese Graded

Level 1: 300 Characters

卷发公司的案子

Juǎnfà Gōngsī de Ànzi

Sherlock Holmes and the Case of the Curly Haired Company

**based on "Sherlock Holmes and the Case of the Red Headed League"
by Sir Arthur Conan Doyle**

Mind Spark Press LLC

SHANGHAI

Published by Mind Spark Press LLC

Shanghai, China

Mandarin Companion is a trademark of Mind Spark Press LLC.

For information about educational or bulk purchases, please contact
Mind Spark Press at business@mandarincompanion.com.

Instructor and learner resources and traditional Chinese editions of
the Mandarin Companion series are available at
www.MandarinCompanion.com.

First paperback print edition March, 2015

Library of Congress Cataloging-in-Publication Data
Doyle, Arthur Conan.
Sherlock Holmes and the Case of the Curly Haired Company : Mandarin Companion
Graded Readers: Level 1, Simplified Chinese Edition / Arthur Conan Doyle,
Renjun Yang; [edited by] John Pasden, Cui Yu.
1st paperback edition.
alt Lake City, UT; Shanghai, China: Mind Spark Press LLC, 2015

LCCN: 2015901609

ISNB: 9781941875018
ISBN: 9780991005246 (ebook)
ISBN: 9780991005260 (ebook/traditional ch)

Mandarin Companion Graded Readers

Now you can read books in Chinese that are fun and help accelerate language learning. Every book in the Mandarin Companion series is carefully written to use characters, words, and grammar that a learner is likely to know.

The Mandarin Companion Leveling System has been meticulously developed through an in-depth analysis of textbooks, education programs and natural Chinese language. Every story is written in a simple style that is fun and easy to understand so you improve with each book.

Mandarin Companion Level 1

Level 1 is intended for Chinese learners at an upper-elementary level. Most learners will be able to approach this book after one to two years of formal study, depending on the learner and program. This series is designed to combine simplicity of characters with an easy-to-understand storyline that helps beginner grow their vocabulary and language comprehension abilities. The more they read, the better they will become at reading and grasping the Chinese language.

Level 1 is designed around the Mandarin Companion's core set of 300 basic characters. These basic characters ensure that most of the vocabulary will be simple everyday words that the reader is most likely to know. This series contains approximately 400 unique words; a number low enough to make reading Chinese less intimidating, while also introducing new key words relevant to the story.

Key words are added gradually over the course of the story. A numbered footnote indicates the first time a new word or character is introduced and the corresponding hyperlink references the glossary with pinyin and an English definition. Each additional instance of a new word is indicated by a hyperlink. All proper nouns have been underlined to help the reader distinguish between names and words.

What level is right for me?

If you are able to read this book with a high level of comprehension, then this book is likely at your level. It is ideal to have at most only one unknown word or character for every 40-50 words or characters that are read.

Once you are able to read fluidly and quickly without interruption you are ready for the next level. Even if you are able to understand all of the words in the book, we recommend that readers build fluidity and reading speed before moving to higher levels.

How will this help my Chinese?

Reading extensively in a language you are learning is one of the most effective ways to build fluency. However, the key is to read at a high level of comprehension. Reading at the appropriate level in Chinese will increase the speed of character recognition, help acquire vocabulary faster, allow readers to naturally learn grammar, and train the brain to think in Chinese. It also makes learning Chinese more fun and enjoyable. Readers will experience the sense of accomplishment and confidence that only comes from reading entire books in Chinese.

Extensive Reading

After years of studying Chinese, many people ask, "why can't I become fluent in Chinese?" Fluency can only happen when the language enters our "comfort zone." This comfort comes after significant exposure to and experience with the language. The more times you meet a word, phrase, or grammar point the more readily it will enter your comfort zone.

In the world of language research, experts agree that learners can acquire new vocabulary through reading only if the overall text can be understood. Decades of research indicate that if we know approximately 98% of the words in a book, we can comfortably "pick up" the 2% that is unfamiliar. Reading at this 98% comprehension level is referred to as "extensive reading."

Research in extensive reading has shown that it accelerates vocabulary learning and helps the learner to naturally understand grammar. Perhaps most importantly, it trains the brain to automatically recognize familiar language, thereby freeing up mental energy to focus on meaning and ideas. As they build reading speed and fluency, learners will move from reading "word by word" to processing "chunks of language." A defining feature is that it's lesspainful than the "intensive reading" commonly used in textbooks. In fact, extensive reading can be downright fun.

Graded Readers

Graded readers are the best books for learners to "extensively" read. Research has taught us that learners need to "encounter" a word 10-30 times before truly learning it, and often many more times for particularly complicated or abstract words. Graded readers are appropriate for learners because the language is controlled and simplified, as opposed to the language in native texts, which is inevitably difficult and often demotivating. Reading extensively with graded readers allows learners to bring together all of the language they have studied and absorb how the words naturally work together.

To become fluent, learners must not only understand the meaning of a word, but also understand its nuances, how to use it in conversation, how to pair it with other words, where it fits into natural word order, and how it is used in grammar structures. No textbook could ever be written to teach all of this explicitly. When used properly, a textbook introduces the language and provides the basic meanings, while graded readers consolidate, strengthen, anddeepen understanding.

Without graded readers, learners would have to study dictionaries, textbooks, sample dialogs, and simple conversations until they have randomly encountered enough Chinese for it to enter their comfort zones. With proper use of graded readers, learners can tackle this issue and develop greater fluency now, at their current levels, instead of waiting until some period in the distant future. With a stronger foundation and greater confidence at their current levels, learners are encouraged and motivated to continue their Chinese studies to even greater heights. Plus, they'll quickly learn that reading Chinese is fun!

Table of Contents

Story Adaptation Notes

This story is an adaptation of Sir Arthur Conan Doyle's 1891 Sherlock Holmes story, "The Red-Headed League." This Mandarin Companion graded reader has been adapted into a fully localized Chinese version of the original story. The characters have been given authentic Chinese names as opposed to transliterations of English names, which sound foreign in Chinese. The locations have been adapted to well-known places in China.

The location has been adapted from Victorian London, England to 1920's Shanghai, China. During this period, Shanghai was known as "The Paris of the East, the New York of the West". It became the focal point of many activities that would eventually shape modern China. The architectural style of many grand buildings built during this period were modeled after British and American designs to suit the preferences of the influential Western businessmen. This time period of Shanghai parallels the period of Victorian London.

The original story involves a group of red-headed males however there are no native Chinese with this hair color. To suit the purposes of the story, we changed "red-headed" to "curly haired" since Chinese with curly hair are about as uncommon as red-heads are in the Western world.

Character Adaptations

The following is a list of the characters from this Chinese story followed by their corresponding English names from Sir Arthur Conan Doyle's original Sherlock Holmes story. The names below are not translations, they are new Chinese names used for the Chinese versions of the original characters. Think of them as all-new characters in a Chinese story.

高明 (Gāo Míng) - Sherlock Holmes

赵亮 (Zhào Liàng) - Doctor Watson

谢先生 (Xiè Xiānsheng) - Jabez Wilson

刘路飞 (Liú Lùfēi) - Vincent Spaulding

卷发公司的老板 (Juǎnfà Gōngsī de Lǎobǎn) - Duncan Ross/William Morris

万经理 (Wàn Jīnglǐ) - Mr. Merryweather

老王 (Lǎo Wáng) - Peter Jones

Cast of Characters

高明
(Gāo Míng)

赵亮
(Zhào Liàng)

谢先生
(Xiè Xiānshēng)

刘路飞
(Liú Lùfēi)

公司的老板
(Gōngsī de Lǎobǎn)

万先生
(Wàn Xiānshēng)

老王
(Lǎo Wáng)

Locations

上海 Shànghǎi

Known as "The Paris of the East, the New York of the West", 1920's Shanghai was a bustling center of commerce and western influence in pre-modern China. Today it is the center of business in modern day China.

外滩 Wàitān

The Bund in Shanghai, a row of grand buildings modeled after British and American architectural styles lining the west bank of the Huangpu River.

— Chapter 1 —
有意思的案子

一个星期五的上午，天气很好。

高明一边吃早饭一边看那天的报纸，可

是他觉得很没意思，因为他很长时间没

有处理案子了。赵亮不想看报纸， 他

想一个人出去走走。中午，赵亮回来的

时候，看到高明在跟一个男人说话。现

在，高明看起来很高兴，话很多，跟

上午很不一样。赵亮又看了一下那个男

人，不高，有点儿胖，最有意思的是，

他的头发是卷的。"头发这么卷的男人，

---

1 报纸 (bàozhǐ) *n.* newspaper

2 处理 (chǔlǐ) *v.* to handle, to deal with

3 案子 (ànzi) *n.* (criminal or legal) case

4 跟...一样 (gēn... yīyàng) *phrase* the same as...

5 有意思 (yǒuyìsi) *adj.* interesting

6 头发 (tóufa) *n.* hair

我从来没有看到过。有意思！"赵亮想。

这个时候，高明也看到了赵亮。他笑着对赵亮说："来，小赵。我这里有一个新案子，你一定想听一下。"说完，他对那个卷发男人说："谢先生，这是我的朋友赵亮。他会跟我一起处理你的案子。"那个男人看了看赵亮，好像不太相信赵亮。

"谢先生，你再多说一点你的案子吧。我很少听说这么奇怪的事。现在，我还不知道你的案子是不是跟别的案子有关。"高明又对卷发男人说。

---

7 从来没有 (cóngláiméiyǒu) *phrase* usual; to have never (done something)

8 一定 (yīdìng) *adv.* surely, certainly

9 卷发 (juǎnfà) *n.* curly hair

10 好像 (hǎoxiàng) *v.* to seem that

11 相信 (xiāngxìn) *v.* to believe

12 奇怪 (qíguài) *adj.* strange

13 跟...有关 (gēn... yǒuguān) *phrase* about..., related to...

　　卷发男人慢慢地拿出了一张报纸。
这个时候，赵亮又认真地看了一下这个
人。他很想跟高明一样，很快就可以知
道这个人是做什么的。可是，赵亮又看
了一会儿，还是不知道这个男人是做什
么的。

---

14 认真 (rènzhēn) *adj.* earnest, serious

高明好像知道赵亮在想什么，马上问卷发男人："谢先生，你是茶馆老板吧？你以前是不是在饭店工作过？还有，你是不是去过海南？"

"你怎么知道？我没告诉过你啊！"卷发男人没想到高明知道这些事。

高明马上笑了，对他说："你的身上有茶的味道。如果不是每天都在茶馆里，就不可能会有这样的味道。你看你的左手，上面有一些伤口，经常用刀的人才会有这样的伤口。还有，我去过海南，你手上的这个东西，只有海南才有。"

---

15 茶馆 (cháguǎn) *n.* teahouse
16 老板 (lǎobǎn) *n.* boss
17 饭店 (fàndiàn) *n.* restaurant
18 味道 (wèidao) *n.* scent, flavor
19 伤口 (shāngkǒu) *n.* wound, cut
20 刀 (dāo) *n.* knife

赵亮一下子不知道应该说什么。他以前总是听别人说高明聪明，这次他真的知道了。卷发男人笑了，他对高明说："我真没想到你都说对了！别人都说这样的案子应该找你，现在，我真的相信了！"

21 应该 (yīnggāi) *aux.* should, ought to   23 聪明 (cōngming) *adj.* smart
22 总是 (zǒngshì) *adv.* always

高明也笑了，说："那个广告是不是
在这张报纸上？你能给我看一下吗？"

"对。就是这张。"卷发男人一边
说，一边给高明那张报纸

---

24 广告 (guǎnggào) *n.* advertisement

Chapter 2
一个广告

高明拿着报纸，先看了一下报纸的时间，是1921年10月7日，已经两个月了。然后，他看到报纸的左边有一个广告：

新新卷发公司现在需要一个卷发助理。每天工作六个小时，一个月七百块。如果你是一个卷发男人，身体好，就可以来天平路100号面试。

赵亮也看了一下这个广告，他觉得这是一个奇怪的广告，但是又不知道哪里奇怪。

---

25 需要 (xūyào) *v.* to need

26 助理 (zhùlǐ) *n.* assistant

27 百 (bǎi) *num.* hundred

28 面试 (miànshì) *v.* to interview

　　高明对赵亮说："小赵，你帮我记一
下报纸的名字和时间。"然后他又对谢先
生说："好了，谢先生，请你说说你为什
么要给我们看这个广告吧。"

　　"你刚才说对了，我在南京路上开
了一个茶馆。那是一个小生意。开茶馆
不会有很多钱。以前有两个人帮我，但

---

29 记 (jì) *v.* to make a note, to write down

30 刚才 (gāngcái) *tn.* just now

31 生意 (shēngyi) *n.* business

是因为生意不好，现在只有一个人帮我了。为了学做茶馆生意，那个男人只要一半的钱。"谢先生慢慢说。

"那个男人叫什么名字？"高明问。

"他叫刘路飞，25岁了，很聪明。我知道，他可以有更好的工作，有更多的钱。可是，他很想来我的茶馆工作，还只要一半的钱，我为什么不要他呢？"谢先生说。

高明笑了，他说："真的吗？只让老板给一半的钱？我从来没有听说过这样奇怪的人。这个叫刘路飞的人跟这个卷发公司的广告一样奇怪。"

---

32 为了 (wèile) *prep.* in order to, for the purpose of

"但是他也有一个问题。"谢先生马

上说，"他太喜欢拍照了，每天都在茶馆

外面拍很多照片，拍完以后马上回茶馆
___33___   ___15___

的地下室洗照片。这是他最大的问题。
___34___   ___15___

但是他工作的时候很不错。"
___35___ ___36___

___37___

33 拍照 (pāizhào) *vo.* to take a photo   36 洗照片 (xǐ zhàopiàn) *vo.* to
34 照片 (zhàopiàn) *n.* photograph   develop photographs
35 地下室 (dìxiàshì) *n.* basement,   37 不错 (bùcuò) *adj.* pretty good,
underground room   not bad

10

听到这里，赵亮觉得更奇怪了，他问谢先生："茶馆里只有你和刘路飞两个人吗？"

"对，只有他在这里工作。"谢先生说，"我也没有别的家人。"

高明又问谢先生："那你能告诉我，你是怎么知道这个广告的？"

"是刘路飞告诉我的。"谢先生马上说，"两个月以前，上午的时候茶馆里没有人，他又出去拍照了。他回来的时候，很开心地给我这张报纸，让我看这个广告。他还说，'我多么希望我也是卷发！'"

38 希望 (xīwàng) *v.* to wish, to hope

高明又问："他让你去卷发公司面试吗？"

谢先生说："对。他说这个新新卷发公司有一个很好的工作，这个工作需要一个卷发的助理。"

"这么奇怪的工作！"赵亮说。

"更奇怪的是，这个工作的钱也不少。一个月七百块。你们知道，我的茶馆生意不好，我真的需要钱。"谢先生说。

"那你去面试了？"高明问。

"对。开始的时候，我觉得那个卷发公司不一定会要我。但是刘路飞说中

---

39 开始 (kāishǐ) *v.; n.* to start　　40 不一定 (bùyīdìng) *adv.* not necessarily

国的卷发男人很少。还有，他说我30岁了，身体也不错，可能很多卷发的男人都太老了，身体也不好。"谢先生说。

高明觉得很有意思，说："那就请你跟我们说说面试的事吧。"

— Chapter 3 —
新工作

    谢先生坐在那里，看着手里的报纸。他想了一会儿，然后说："我以后不想去面试这样的工作了。那么多卷发的男人都去那里面试。如果不是因为这个面试，我都不知道上海有这么多卷发男人。他们的头发，有的不太卷，有的很卷。但是，像刘路飞说的那样，他们很多都是身体不太好的老人，他们都想要这个工作。那么多卷发的人来面试，我觉得他们不一定会要我。我也不喜欢去人多的地方。想到这些，我有点儿想回家了。"

"那后来呢？"高明马上问。

"但是刘路飞不同意。他一定让我去试一试。"谢先生又说，"他带我慢慢地往办公室走。快到办公室的时候，我们看到一些人很开心地往办公室里走，还有一些人很难过地从办公室里出来。很快，我们也在办公室里了。"

41 后来 (hòulái) *tn.* afterwards

42 同意 (tóngyì) *v.* to agree (with)

43 试 (shì) *v.* to try

44 难过 (nánguò) *adj.* sad, upset

"怎么样？你是他们想找的人吗？"赵亮很想知道后面的事。

"你听我慢慢说。"谢先生不太喜欢赵亮，他觉得赵亮总是问很多问题。他喝了一点茶，然后说，"他们的办公室很奇怪，只有一个大桌子和几个椅子，没有别的东西。他们的老板也是一个卷发男人，他坐在椅子上，每一个卷发男人都要走到桌子前，跟老板说话。但是那个老板总是能找到那些卷发男人的问题，然后让他们出去。但是…"

"但是什么？"赵亮又问。

"我走过去的时候，刘路飞对他说，'这是我的老板谢先生，他希望在这

45 桌子 (zhuōzi) *n.* table, desk
46 椅子 (yǐzi) *n.* chair
47 找到 (zhǎodào) *vc.* to find

16

里做助理。'刘路飞刚说完，那个老板一
下子很开心。他马上对我说，'太好了！
你就是我们要找的助理。你的头发又黑
又卷，很漂亮。'然后他走到门外，对别
的来面试的人说，'你们可以回去了，我
已经找到最好的助理了。'"

48 漂亮 (piàoliang) *adj.* pretty

高明笑了一下，对谢先生说："对你来说，找到这个工作一点也不难。"

"对。"谢先生说，"他们让我第二天就去上班。每天上午八点到下午两点，工作是看书、写东西。可是，我想到我还要开茶馆，可能没办法在这个时间上班。这个时候，刘路飞马上说，'放心吧，老板。平常下午三点以后才有人来茶馆。再说，我一直都在茶馆里。'听他这么说，我马上同意第二天就去上班。"

"这么奇怪的面试！我真想听你说说你在新新卷发公司做什么。"高明说。他

---

49 一点也 (yīdiǎnyě) *phrase* (not) at all
50 上班 (shàngbān) *vo.* to go to work
51 放心 (fàngxīn) *vo.* to relax, to rest assured
52 平常 (píngcháng) *adv.; adj.* ordinarily; ordinary
53 再说 (zàishuō) *conj.* and besides
54 一直 (yīzhí) *adv* all along, continuously

觉得这个案子越来越有意思了。

　　"我从来没有听说过这么奇怪的公司，也从来没有做过这么奇怪的工作，我相信你们的想法也跟我一样。"谢先生坐在椅子上，慢慢地说。

---

55 越来越… (yuèláiyuè…) *adv.* more and more…
56 想法 (xiǎngfa) *n.* idea, way of thinking

Chapter 4
公司关门了？

　　高明和赵亮都很认真地听谢先生说他的案子，但是一直到现在，赵亮还是不知道哪里有问题。

　　"谢先生，你能告诉我们你在新新卷发公司的工作怎么样吗？"高明问。

　　"从第一天开始，我就觉得很奇怪。"谢先生又拿起桌子上的茶，喝了一点。"我第一天去上班的时候，发现他们的办公室只有两个人。一个是那天面试我的老板，还有一个人我不认识。办公室里什么都没有，只有那个大桌子和几个椅子，桌子上有很多书。老板告诉我，'从今天开始，你就坐在这里工作。你是助理，你的工作就是看这些书，然后写一些你的想法。还有，你写的想法应该跟卷发有关。'"

"真奇怪！"赵亮说。

"还有更奇怪的事。"谢先生说，"那个老板又说，'你不能走出这个办公室。上班的六个小时里，你都要在这里，不能出去。如果你出去了，你就没有这个工作了。'我问他，'那我吃午饭怎么办？'没想到老板告诉我，那个我不认识的人会和我一起在办公室里，他会帮我买午饭。"

听到这里，高明又笑了，他说："我相信，从来没有人做过这样的工作。你不觉得这个公司有问题吗？"

"我早就觉得有问题了。"谢先生有点生气，他不想让别人觉得他不聪明，他说："所以那天下午回到茶馆以后，我很不开心。我告诉刘路飞，我觉得那个公司一定有问题。没有公司会给一个助理那么多钱，让他每天坐在办公室里，只看书、写没用的东西。但是刘路飞让我不要想太多，他说那么多人去面试，只有我一个人有这个机会。他还说七百块钱真的不少。我觉得他说得对，因为对我来说，我真的需要那些钱。"

---

58 生气 (shēngqì) *adj.; v.* angry; to get angry

59 没用 (méiyòng) *adj.* useless

60 机会 (jīhuì) *n.* opportunity

"那你为什么告诉我们？"赵亮问。

"我以为我可以一直在那个卷发公司工作，每个月拿七百块钱。"谢先生看起来很难过，他说，"可是就在昨天，我去上班的时候，发现公司已经关门了。门上有一张纸，上面写着：

新新卷发公司已经关门！

听到这里，高明和赵亮一下子笑了。谢先生很生气，对他们大叫："很好笑吗？如果你们只会笑我，不会做别的事，我可以去别的地方。"说完，他就从椅子上起来了。

---

61 大叫 (dàjiào) v. to yell, to loudly cry out

62 好笑 (hǎoxiào) adj. funny

63 笑 (xiào) v. to laugh at (someone)

"不，不。"高明一边说，一边让谢先生坐下。"我真的很想处理你这个案子，它太有意思了。如果你不生气的话，我还是想说，你说的事真的很好笑。我想知道公司关门以后，你做了什么？"

"我马上去问了一些住在天平路上的人，可是他们从来没有听说过这个新新卷发公司，也不知道那个老板是谁。没有别的办法，我只能回到茶馆。刘路飞说了很多话，让我别难过。我怎么会不难过？在那里工作的时候，我每个月可以有七百块钱。可是现在我没有工作了，钱跟以前一样少了。"

"好了，别难过了。你工作了两个月，他们给了你两个月的钱。很好啊！你在那里工作的时候，你也看了很多书啊。"高明说，"可是，我觉得你的案子可能跟别的大案子有关。"

— Chapter 5 —
茶馆里的事

高明说谢先生的案子可能跟别的大案子有关，这是赵亮没想到的，赵亮也不知道高明为什么会这样想。

这个时候，高明从椅子上起来，他在房间里走来走去，好像在想什么事。过了一会儿，他问谢先生："谢先生，刘路飞在你的茶馆里工作了多长时间了？"

"三个月了。"谢先生说。

"他怎么知道你需要别人帮你做生意？"高明又问。

"三个月以前，他到了我的茶馆，告诉我他很想学做这个生意。为了让我同意，他还告诉我他不需要我每个月给他很多钱。"谢先生说。

"他是个什么样的人？"高明问。

"他不高，但是身体很好，也很聪明。只是他的左手有点小问题。"谢先生说。

高明很开心地坐在了椅子上，他问谢先生："他的左手上是不是有一个长长的伤口？"

"是的。"谢先生没想到高明知道这个。

"你不在的时候，他一直在茶馆里帮你做生意吗？"高明好像知道了什么。

"对。他很聪明，他帮我做生意我很放心。再说，茶馆生意不好，三点以前，茶馆里人很少。"谢先生说。

"好了。我知道了。今天是星期五，下个星期一以前我会处理完这个案子。"高明看起来越来越开心。

谢先生走了以后，高明问赵亮："对这个案子，你有什么想法？"

赵亮笑了一下，不好意思地说："我同意你的看法，我也觉得这个案子很奇怪。但是我不知道哪里奇怪。"

高明说："那些看起来很奇怪的案子，到了知道真相的时候，你就会发现它们没那么奇怪。那些看起来很平常的案子有可能有更大的问题。现在，我们要马上处理这个案子。"

"那我们应该怎么做？"赵亮问。

"我要认真想一下。从现在开始，请你在一个小时里都不要跟我说话。"

说完，高明坐在椅子上，开始想这个案

---

64 不好意思 (bùhǎoyìsi) *adj.*
embarrassed, "I'm sorry, but..."

65 真相 (zhēnxiàng) *n.* the true situation

子。赵亮也坐在椅子上看着高明，他不知道高明在想什么，也不知道自己应该做什么。坐了很长时间，赵亮有点儿想睡觉了。可是，就在这个时候，高明一下子从椅子上起来了，他对赵亮说："走，我们去南京路。希望能有一些发现。"

— Chapter 6 —
去茶馆

很快，高明和赵亮就来到了南京路。南京路是上海最有名的路，路上有很多店。从南京路一直往东走，就可以走到外滩。

走了一会儿，高明和赵亮就来到了一个茶馆前面。这个茶馆跟别的店不一样，它很小，里面有点黑。如果不认真看，路上的人很难看到这个茶馆。茶馆外面有四个大字：老谢茶馆。

"这一定是谢先生的茶馆。我们进去看看吧？"赵亮对高明说。

67 外滩 (Wàitān) *n.* the Bund (in Shanghai)

"等一下。不要马上进去。"高明
说。然后他走到茶馆右边不远的地方，
拿起一块石头在地面上敲了几下，一边
敲一边听。赵亮觉得很奇怪，他不知道
高明在做什么。

过了一会儿，高明对赵亮说："走
吧，我们进茶馆看看。"

高明和赵亮刚进去，一个男人就笑着走过来。他二十多岁，不高，但是看起来很聪明，他的左手上有一个很长的伤口。高明和赵亮知道：这个人就是刘路飞。

"请问你们要喝什么茶？"刘路飞问高明和赵亮。

高明也笑了一下，说："不好意思，我们不喝茶。我们想问一下，从这里去外滩应该怎么走？"

"出门以后一直往右走，你们就会看到外滩。"刘路飞说。

"好的。谢谢！"高明说完，就和赵亮一起从茶馆里出来了。

　　高明一边走一边说："刘路飞看起

来是一个很聪明的人。我以前就听说过

这个人，这次有机会看到他，更让我相

信，这个案子一定跟更大的案子有关。"

　　"我知道你去茶馆就是为了看刘路

飞。"赵亮说。

"我不是为了看他，是为了去看他的鞋。"高明说。

"啊？鞋？你看到了什么？"赵亮觉得很奇怪。

"我看到了我想看的东西。"高明说。

"那你为什么要用石头在地面上敲几下？"赵亮又问。

"你很快就会知道了。"高明笑了一下。

很快，高明和赵亮就到了外滩。高明对赵亮说："你看，外滩在中山路上。在南京路上一直走，很快就可以到中山路。 从谢先生的茶馆到外滩，有两个饭店、一个书店、一个小吃店，还有一个大银行。"

"你为什么要看这些？"赵亮问。

"以后你就会知道，这很重要。"高明说，"这个案子很可能是一个大案子。"

"为什么是一个大案子呢？"赵亮又问。

"很快你就会知道了。但是我相信我很快会处理完这个案子。今天晚上，我想请你帮我一下。"高明说。

"好啊。什么时候？"赵亮问。

---

73 书店 (shūdiàn) *n.* book store　　74 银行 (yínháng) *n.* bank

"你先回家吧。我还要去处理一下别的事。我们十点在家见面吧。还有，今天晚上的事很重要，请你记得带你的枪。"说完，高明就走了。

— Chapter 7 —
你们听！

　　在回家的路上，赵亮一直在想："以前我总是觉得自己很聪明。可是我和高明一起工作以后，就不这样想了。谢先生的案子，高明听到的我都听到了，他看到的我也都看到了。可是，他什么都知道，我什么都不知道。为什么我什么都不知道？"赵亮又从最开始想谢先生的案子。从谢先生去面试卷发公司的工作，到卷发公司关门；从高明用石头在地面上敲了几下，到去茶馆看刘路飞。

对赵亮来说，他还是不知道哪里奇怪。

"高明为什么要十点见面？为什么让我带枪去？他要做什么？"赵亮想。可是他想了很长时间还是不知道。"我想这么多也没用，到了晚上就知道了。"赵亮又想。

快十点的时候，高明回来了。过了一会儿，又来了两个男人。赵亮认识那个很高的男人。他是上海有名的警察老王，经常请高明帮忙处理一些很难很奇怪的案子。

高明看到老王的时候，马上说："小赵，这是老王，你还记得吧？"

---

77 警察 (jǐngchá) *n.* police officer, the police

"记得。这是…?"赵亮看了一下老王身边的男人。

"这是中国银行的经理万先生。他们会和我们一起处理谢先生的案子。"高明说。

"万经理?银行?谢先生的案子怎么跟银行有关?"赵亮想。

万经理好像不那么相信高明,他说:"我希望今晚能处理完这个案子。今天晚上我应该跟家人在一起,但是为了这个案子,我现在跟你们在一起。"

"你不相信高明吗?"老王问,"对高明来说,没有不能处理的案子,我们警察都知道。"

赵亮也有点生气，他说："老王说得对。再说，你已经来了，还不相信高明？那你为什么来？"

"好了，时间不早了，我们走吧。"高明说。

然后，这四个人就坐上了万经理的车，去了中国银行。很快，他们就到了外滩。中国银行就在外滩，但是，跟下午不一样，现在这里人很少。

他们下车以后，万经理就带他们进了银行。万经理拿着一个灯，走在前面。他先开了一个小门，四个人进去以后，走了一会儿；然后，他又开了一个大门，从大门进去以后，他们又往地下室走；然后，万经理又开了最后一个门，他们就进了银行的地下室。地下室里的味道很奇怪，赵亮很不喜欢。

78 灯 (dēng) *n.* a light

赵亮看了看地下室，这里有很多大箱子，但是他不知道箱子里面有什么。赵亮还发现地下室没有别的门，如果不是万经理带他们来，就没有人能进来。

所以赵亮一边看一边说："别人想从上面到这个地下室是很难的。"

万经理高兴地笑了，他拿起一块石头，在地面上敲了几下，一边敲，一边说："对！想从上面到地下室是很难的，想从下面到这里也是很难的。"可是很快，他又大叫："啊！你们听！这里的地下是空的！"

— Chapter 8 —
等人

　　高明看起来一点也不觉得奇怪，好像他已经知道了这个真相。他有点儿生气地对万经理说："你不要大叫！你这样做会让他们发现我们的。我请你们现在就坐在那些箱子上，都别说话。"

　　万经理有点不开心，因为很少有人对他这样说话。但是没有别的办法，现在，他需要听高明的。然后，那三个人都坐在了那些大箱子上。

这个时候，高明小心地拿着灯，认真地看着地面。赵亮觉得高明好像发现了什么。高明一边看一边说："这里的地面真的有问题。跟我想的一样！"然后，他对那三个人说："我们还要再等一个小时，因为谢先生睡觉以前，那些人是不会做什么的。谢先生睡了以后，他们就会很快进来，拿他们想要的东西。"说完，他又看着赵亮，对他说："小赵，你已经知道了，现在我们在中国银行的地下室里。万经理会告诉你，为什么那些人会想办法来这个地下室。"

万经理说："他们就是为了我们银行的黄金。"

---

81 小心 (xiǎoxīn) *v.* to be careful   82 黄金 (huángjīn) *n.* gold

"黄金？"赵亮问。

"对。几个月以前，五十箱黄金从南京的银行到了这里。那些人知道以后，一直想从这个地下室里拿走黄金。现在，你坐的箱子里面都是黄金。"万经理说。

高明说："我们现在开始想想怎么做吧。我觉得我们一个小时以后就会知道这个案子的真相了。现在，我要关灯，等那些想拿走黄金的人进来。"

"我们要在这么黑的地下室里等吗？"万经理说。

"是的。如果不关灯，他们很快就会发现我们。"高明说，"现在，你们每个人都去一个箱子的后面。万经理，请你在这个箱子后面，拿着灯，一会儿他们进来的时候，你就开灯，我和小赵、老王会抓住他们。记住，他们可能带了枪，如果他们开枪，我们也要马上开枪。"

说完以后，高明就关了灯，他们四个人都到了四个箱子的后面。地下室一

83 抓住 (zhuāzhù) *vc.* to catch   84 开枪 (kāiqiāng) *vo.* to fire a gun

下子黑了，他们什么都看不见了。

"他们没有别的路可以逃，只能逃到谢先生的茶馆里，从那里跑出去。老王，我让你做的事，你已经做好了吧？"高明问警察老王。

"放心吧。我已经让三个警察等在茶馆外面了。希望不会再让他们逃了。"老王说。赵亮很奇怪为什么老王说"再让他们逃了"。可是他没有时间问。

时间过得很慢。赵亮很紧张。在地下室里的那一个多小时，对赵亮来说，好像是一个晚上。

一个多小时以后，好像真的有人来了。

— Chapter 9 —
真的是他!

对，真的有人来了！

高明、赵亮、万经理和王警察都在箱子后面，从他们的地方往前看，什么都看不到。可是，很快，他们就发现了刚刚那块地面下有一些灯光。在那么黑的地下室里，一点点灯光也可以很快发现。这个时候，赵亮很紧张。可是，过了一会儿，那些灯光没有了。他们又等了一会儿，地下的灯光又有了。然后，他们就看到有人打开了地面的那块石

---

86 灯光 (dēngguāng) *n.* lamplight 87 打开 (dǎkāi) *vc.* to open

头。有一个人拿着灯，往地下室里看了

一下，从下面出来了。

　　"啊！刘路飞！"赵亮在心里大叫。

看到刘路飞，他更紧张了。"真的是

他！"赵亮现在才知道，高明说的更大的

案子就是银行的这个案子。

　　刘路飞进了地下室以后，没有马上

去拿箱子里的黄金。他在那里帮别的人

进地下室。很快，第二个人也进来了。

他不高，头发也是卷的。"这个人很可能

就是面试谢先生的卷发公司的老板。"赵

亮想。

　　第二个人进来以后，小心地对刘路

飞说："我们需要的东西都带进来了，快

开始吧…"他还没说完，箱子后面的万经

理就开了灯。这个时候，高明和赵亮很

快跑过去，抓住了刘路飞。

"不好！快跑…"刘路飞还没说完，第二个人就看到他们了，想回到地下室下面，可是已经晚了，老王抓住了他。

"不要跑！现在跑没用了。警察已经在外面等你们了。刘路飞，我已经找了你们两个人很长时间了。"高明对刘路飞说。

"啊！你们两个人就是今天来茶馆问路的人？"刘路飞看了一下高明和赵亮，问他们。

"对。我们又见面了！卷发公司的想法真有意思。"高明说。

"你们放开我，我自己可以走。"刘路飞生气地大叫。

这个时候，万经理走过来，对刘路飞说："你真是一个聪明的人。为了拿走银行的黄金，想了这么多办法。可是最后，这些黄金还是在银行里。你们快上去吧，警察在等你们。"

从地下室出来以后，万经理对高明说："我真不知道应该怎么谢谢你们。我在银行工作这么多年了，但是从来没有看到过有人想用这种方法拿走黄金。你们用最聪明的方法抓住了他们，我真的应该谢谢你们！"

高明说："我跟老王找了刘路飞很长时间了，他还跟别的案子有关。我也应该谢谢你给我这个机会抓住了他。我相信，我的朋友也从这个案子里学到了很多东西。"说完，高明看了一下赵亮，笑了。赵亮也明白了为什么老王要说"再让他们逃了"这样的话，他也看了一下高明，笑了。

—— Chapter 10 ——
都明白了

现在这个案子有了真相。在回家的路上，高明和赵亮一边走，一边说刚才的案子。

高明对赵亮说："小赵，你看，发现这个案子的真相不难，从开始的时候就不难。新新卷发公司那个奇怪的广告，和那个钱很多、事很少的工作，我可以发现他们的目的只有一个，就是让谢先生每天有几个小时不在茶馆里。这个办法很好笑，但是他们很难再想出别的更好的办法。刘路飞真的很聪明，他知道谢先生一定会觉得奇怪，但是为了每个月七百块钱，谢先生一定会这样做。为了拿到黄金，刘路飞一定会觉得七百块钱一点也不多。他们找了一个办公室，然后在报纸上做广告，然后刘路飞让谢先生去面试。从我听到刘路飞只要一半

89 目的 (mùdì) *n.* purpose, motive

的钱开始，我就知道他一定有目的。"

"可是，你怎么知道他的目的是什么呢？"赵亮问。

"谢先生的茶馆是一个小生意，也没有很多钱，所以，茶馆一定不是他们的目的。"高明说，"但是，谢先生说刘路飞喜欢拍照，经常去地下室洗照片。地下室！那么长时间，他在地下室还能做什么？还有，什么事需要在地下室里做两个月？我想只能是跟地道有关。"

"你用石头在地面上敲了几下，就是想听听下面是不是空的？"赵亮问。

"我知道一定有地道。我用石头敲地面，就是为了知道地道在哪里。"高明

90 地道 (dìdào) *n.* tunnel

说，"我们进茶馆的时候，我看到刘路飞的鞋，这让我更相信自己的想法是对的。每天在地道里的人才会这样。后来，我还想知道的是，他们要这个地道做什么？"

"你怎么知道的？"赵亮问。

"你还记得我让你看从南京路到外滩有哪些店吗？我发现银行后门不远的地方，就是谢先生的茶馆。你回家的时候，我就去银行跟万经理见面了。后面的事，你都看到了。"高明说。

"那你怎么知道他们会在今天晚上进银行地下室呢？"赵亮还是有问题。

高明说："听到新新卷发公司关门的

时候，我就知道刘路飞今天晚上一定会进银行地下室。卷发公司昨天关门了，意思是，对刘路飞来说，谢先生在茶馆还是不在茶馆都不重要了。因为他们的地道已经可以用了。明天是星期六，后天是星期天，银行里的人都不上班。如果今天晚上他们能拿走黄金，没有人会发现黄金不见了。这样，他们就有两天的时间逃到别的地方。"

现在，赵亮什么都知道了。他看着高明，说："人们都说你最聪明，现在我真的相信了！"

高明又笑了，他说："处理案子让我的生活更有意思。我们的生活已经很没意思了，所以一定要多做一些有意思的事。这些小小的案子帮了我。"赵亮笑了，他很同意高明的话。

已经很晚了，路上有点黑。但是赵亮知道，明天马上就要到了。

Key Words 关键词 (Guānjiàncí)

1. 报纸 (bàozhǐ) *n.* newspaper
2. 处理 (chǔlǐ) *v.* to handle, to deal with
3. 案子 (ànzi) *n.* (criminal or legal) case
4. 跟...一样 (gēn... yīyàng) *phrase* the same as...
5. 有意思 (yǒuyìsi) *adj.* interesting
6. 头发 (tóufa) *n.* hair
7. 从来没有 (cóngláiméiyǒu) *phrase* to have never (done something)
8. 一定 (yīdìng) *adv.* surely, certainly
9. 卷发 (juǎnfà) *n.* curly hair
10. 好像 (hǎoxiàng) *v.* to seem that
11. 相信 (xiāngxìn) *v.* to believe
12. 奇怪 (qíguài) *adj.* strange
13. 跟...有关 (gēn... yǒuguān) *phrase* about..., related to...
14. 认真 (rènzhēn) *adj.* earnest, serious
15. 茶馆 (cháguǎn) *n.* teahouse
16. 老板 (lǎobǎn) *n.* boss
17. 饭店 (fàndiàn) *n.* restaurant
18. 味道 (wèidao) *n.* scent, flavor
19. 伤口 (shāngkǒu) *n.* wound, cut
20. 刀 (dāo) *n.* knife
21. 应该 (yīnggāi) *aux.* should, ought to
22. 总是 (zǒngshì) *adv.* always
23. 聪明 (cōngming) *adj.* smart
24. 广告 (guǎnggào) *n.* advertisement
25. 需要 (xūyào) *v.* to need
26. 助理 (zhùlǐ) *n.* assistant
27. 百 (bǎi) *num.* hundred
28. 面试 (miànshì) *v.* to interview
29. 记 (jì) *v.* to make a note, to write down

30. 刚才 (gāngcái) *tn.* just now

31. 生意 (shēngyi) *n.* business

32. 为了 (wèile) *prep.* in order to, for the purpose of

33. 拍照 (pāizhào) *vo.* to take a photo

34. 照片 (zhàopiàn) *n.* photograph

35. 地下室 (dìxiàshì) *n.* basement, underground room

36. 洗照片 (xǐ zhàopiàn) *vo.* to develop photographs

37. 不错 (bùcuò) *adj.* pretty good, not bad

38. 希望 (xīwàng) *v.* to wish, to hope

39. 开始 (kāishǐ) *v.; n.* to start

40. 不一定 (bùyīdìng) *adv.* not necessarily

41. 后来 (hòulái) *tn.* afterwards

42. 同意 (tóngyì) *v.* to agree (with)

43. 试 (shì) *v.* to try

44. 难过 (nánguò) *adj.* sad, upset

45. 桌子 (zhuōzi) *n.* table, desk

46. 椅子 (yǐzi) *n.* chair

47. 找到 (zhǎodào) *vc.* to find

48. 漂亮 (piàoliang) *adj.* pretty

49. 一点也 (yīdiǎnyě) *phrase* (not) at all

50. 上班 (shàngbān) *vo.* to go to work

51. 放心 (fàngxīn) *vo.* to relax, to rest assured

52. 平常 (píngcháng) *adv.; adj.* ordinarily; ordinary

53. 再说 (zàishuō) *conj.* and besides

54. 一直 (yīzhí) *adv.* all along, continuously

55. 越来越... (yuèláiyuè...) *adv.* more and more...

56. 想法 (xiǎngfa) *n.* idea, way of thinking

57. 发现 (fāxiàn) *v.* to discover

58. 生气 (shēngqì) *adj.; v.* angry; to get angry

59. 没用 (méiyòng) *adj.* useless

60. 机会 (jīhuì) *n.* opportunity

61. 大叫 (dàjiào) *v.* to yell, to loudly cry out

62. 好笑 (hǎoxiào) *adj.* funny

63. 笑 (xiào) *v.* to laugh at (someone)

64. 不好意思 (bùhǎoyìsi) *adj.* embarrassed, "I'm sorry, but..."

65. 真相 (zhēnxiàng) *n.* the true situation

66. 睡觉 (shuìjiào) *vo.* to sleep

67. 外滩 (Wàitān) *n.* the Bund (in Shanghai)

68. 等 (děng) *v.* to wait

69. 石头 (shítou) *n.* rock, stone

70. 地面 (dìmiàn) *n.* the ground

71. 敲 (qiāo) *v.* to knock

72. 鞋 (xié) *n.* shoe

73. 书店 (shūdiàn) *n.* book store

74. 银行 (yínháng) *n.* bank

75. 记得 (jìde) *v.* to remember

76. 枪 (qiāng) *n.* gun

77. 警察 (jǐngchá) *n.* police officer, the police

78. 灯 (dēng) *n.* a light

79. 箱子 (xiāngzi) *n.* box, crate

80. 空的 (kōngde) *adj.* empty

81. 小心 (xiǎoxīn) *v.* to be careful

82. 黄金 (huángjīn) *n.* gold

83. 抓住 (zhuāzhù) *vc.* to catch

84. 开枪 (kāiqiāng) *vo.* to fire a gun

85. 紧张 (jǐnzhāng) *adj.* nervous

86. 灯光 (dēngguāng) *n.* lamplight

87. 打开 (dǎkāi) *vc.* to open

88. 问路 (wènlù) *vo.* to ask the way

89. 目的 (mùdì) *n.* purpose, motive

90. 地道 (dìdào) *n.* tunnel

Part of Speech Key

adj. Adjective

adv. Adverb

aux. Auxiliary Verb

conj. Conjunction

mw. Measure Word

n. Noun

on. Onomatopoeia

part. Particle

pn. Proper Noun

tn. Time Noun

v. Verb

vc. Verb plus Complement

vo. Verb plus Object

Discussion Questions
讨论问题 (Tǎolùn Wèntí)

Chapter 1 有意思的案子

1. 高明不认识谢先生，但是他为什么知道谢先生的很多事?

    他是怎么知道的?

2. 你喜欢什么样头发的男生和女生? 为什么?

3. 如果你有一次机会，你希望你的头发是什么颜色的?

4. 你觉得你的父母或者朋友最不喜欢你有什么颜色的头发? ?

5. 一百多年以前，中国男人的头发都是很长的。你知道为什么后来

    中国男人都是短头发吗?

Chapter 2 一个广告

1. 请说一说你看过的有意思的广告 。

2. 你觉得什么样的工作是好工作?

3. 你听说过什么奇怪的工作吗? 请说一说。

Chapter 3 新工作

1. 如果你是谢先生，刘路飞告诉你那个工作以后，你会去卷发公司

    面试吗? 为什么?

2. 你的第一次面试怎么样? 请说一说。

Chapter 4 公司关门了?

1. 如果有一份工作，你很不喜欢但是会有很多钱，你会不会做? 为什么?

2. 说说你的第一个老板。

Chapter 5 茶馆里的事

1. 如果你是高明，谢先生告诉你所有的事以后，你会想什么？

2. 你以后想自己做老板吗？你想做什么？为什么？

Chapter 6 去茶馆

1. 高明和刘路飞去南京路以后，为什么高明用石头在路面上敲了几下？

2. 你觉得上海怎么样？上海哪里最好玩？

3. 你知道中国哪些有名的地方？你想去吗？为什么？

Chapter 7 你们听！

1. 你听说过像高明一样聪明的人吗？请说一说他的事。

2. 现在在中国，只有警察可以有枪。你同意吗？为什么？

Chapter 8 等人

1. 你怕黑吗？你有没有一个人去过很黑的地方？请你说一说。

2. 你什么时候会很紧张？如果你很紧张，你会怎么做？

Chapter 9 真的是他！

1. 在银行的地下室里，高明抓住刘路飞的时候，你觉得刘路飞在想什么？

2. 小时候，你和你的朋友有没有做过不好的事？请说一说。

Chapter 10 都明白了

1. 在处理案子的时候，赵亮有哪些不明白的地方？请都说一说。

2. 你什么时候最开心？

Appendix A:
Character Comparison Reference

This appendix is designed to help Chinese teachers and learners use the Mandarin Companion Graded Readers as a companion to the most popular university textbooks and the HSK word lists.

The tables below compare the characters and vocabulary used in other study materials with those found in this Mandarin Companion graded reader. The tables below will display the exact characters and vocabulary used in this book and not covered by these sources. A learner who has studied these textbooks will likely find it easier to read this graded reader by focusing on these characters and words.

Integrated Chinese Level 1, Part 1-2 (3rd Ed.)
Words and characters in this story not covered by these two textbooks:

Character	Pinyin	Word(s)	Pinyin
赵	zhào	赵亮	Zhào Liàng
案	àn	案子	ànzi
卷	juǎn	卷发	juǎnfà
刘	liú	刘路飞	Liú Lùfēi
奇	qí	奇怪	qíguài
怪	guài	奇怪	qíguài
万	wàn	万经理	Wàn jīnglǐ
银	yín	银行	yínháng
相	xiāng	相信	xiāngxìn
门	mén	关门 出门	guānmén chūmén
板	bǎn	老板	lǎobǎn

Character	Pinyin	Word(s)	Pinyin
处	chù	处理	chǔlǐ
滩	tān	外滩	Wàitān
需	xū	需要	xūyào
敲	qiāo	敲	qiāo
警	jǐng	警察	jǐngchá
石	shí	石头	shítou
察	chá	警察	jǐngchá
助	zhù	助理	zhùlǐ
逃	táo	逃	táo
抓	zhuā	抓住	zhuāzhù
枪	qiāng	开枪	kāiqiāng
目	mù	目的	mùdì
伤	shāng	伤口	shāngkǒu
总	zǒng	总是	zǒngshì
光	guāng	灯光	dēngguāng
山	shān	中山路	Zhōngshān Lù
刀	dāo	刀	dāo

New Practical Chinese Reader, Books 1-2 (1st Ed.)

Words and characters in this story not covered by these two textbooks:

Character	Pinyin	Word(s)	Pinyin
赵	zhào	赵亮	Zhào Liàng
案	àn	案子	ànzi
卷	juǎn	卷发	juǎnfà
刘	liú	刘路飞	Liú Lùfēi
奇	qí	奇怪	qíguài
怪	guài	奇怪	qíguài
板	bǎn	老板	lǎobǎn
更	gèng	更	gèng
黄	huáng	黄金	huángjīn
灯	dēng	灯光	dēngguāng
处	chǔ	处理	chǔlǐ
椅	yǐ	椅子	yǐzi
滩	tān	外滩	Wàitān
需	xū	需要	xūyào
直	zhí	一直	yīzhí
敲	qiāo	敲	qiāo
班	bān	上班	shàngbān
逃	táo	逃	táo
枪	qiāng	开枪	kāiqiāng
望	wàng	希望	xīwàng
希	xī	希望	xīwàng
紧	jǐn	紧张	jǐnzhāng
味	wèi	味道	wèidao
胖	pàng	胖	pàng

Hanyu Shuiping Kaoshi (HSK) Levels 1-3

The characters and their associated words in this book not covered by the levels above:

Character	Pinyin	Word(s)	Pinyin
赵	zhào	赵亮	Zhào Liàng
案	àn	案子	ànzi
卷	juǎn	卷发	juǎnfà
刘	liú	刘路飞	Liú Lùfēi
王	wáng	老王	lǎo wáng
金	jīn	黄金	huángjīn
处	chù	处理	chǔlǐ
广	guǎng	广告	guǎnggào
滩	tān	外滩	Wàitān
敲	qiāo	敲	qiāo
察	chá	警察	jǐngchá
警	jǐng	警察	jǐngchá
石	shí	石头	shítou
逃	táo	逃	táo
海	hǎi	上海 海南	Shànghǎi Hǎinán
枪	qiāng	开枪	kāiqiāng
抓	zhuā	抓住	zhuāzhù
拍	pāi	拍照	pāizhào
伤	shāng	伤口	shāngkǒu
光	guāng	灯光	dēngguāng
紧	jǐn	紧张	jǐnzhāng
味	wèi	味道	wèidao

Character	Pinyin	Word(s)	Pinyin
活	huó	生活	shēnghuó
刀	dāo	刀	dāo

Appendix B: Grammar Point Index

For learners new to reading in Chinese, an understanding of grammar points can be extremely helpful for learners and teachers. The following is a list of the most challenging grammar points used in this graded reader.

These grammar points correspond to the Common European Framework of Reference for Languages (CEFR) level A2 or above. The full list with explanations and examples of each grammar point can be found on the Chinese Grammar Wiki, the internet's definitive source of information on Chinese grammar.

CHAPTER 1	
Modifying nouns with adjective + "de"	Adj + 的 + N
Modifying nouns with phrase + "de"	(Phrase) + 的 + N
Simultaneous tasks with "yibian"	(一)边 + V, (一)边 + V
Two words for "but"	Statement, 可是/但是 + transitional statement
Explaining causes with "yinwei"	……, 因为…
"Would like to" with "xiang"	想 + V
Explaining results with "suoyi"	……, 所以…
Actions in a row	(Verb Phrase 1) + (Verb Phrase 2)
Verb reduplication with "yi"	Verb + 一 + Verb
At the time when	……的时候
Result complements "dao" and "jian"	V + 到 / 见
Expressing actions in progress	(正)在 + V
Expressing "with" with "gen"	跟…… + V
Appearance with "kanqilai"	看起来……
Again in the past with "you"	又 + V
Expressing "a little too" with "you dian"	有点(儿) + Adj
The "zui" superlative	最 + Adj
Adjectives with "name" and "zheme"	那么 / 这么 + Adj
"Never" with "conglai"	从来不/从来没(有)
Expressing experiences with "guo"	Verb + 过

Expressing completion with "le"	Subject + Verb + 了 + Object
Aspect particle "zhe"	V + 着
Using "dui"	对 + Noun……
Verbing briefly with "yixia"	Verb + 一下
"-wan" result complement	Subject + Verb + 完 + Object
Expressing "together" with "yiqi"	一起 + V
"It seems" with "haoxiang"	好像……
"Not very" with "bu tai"	不太 + Adj
Again in the future with "zai"	再 + V
Doing something more with "duo"	多 + V
Suggestions with "ba"	Command + 吧
Continuation with "hai"	还 + V / Adj
Measure words to differentiate	这 / 那 + MW (+ N)
Reduplication of adjectives	Adj + Adj
Turning adjectives into adverbs	Adj + 地 + V
Direction complement	V (+ Direction) + 来 / 去
Measure words to differentiate	这 / 那 + MW (+ N)
Expressing earliness with "jiu"	就
Expressing duration with "le"	Verb + 了 + Duration
Softening speech with "ba"	Statement + 吧
"Before" in general	以前, ……
Using "zai" with verbs	Subj. + 在 + Place + V
Expressing "in addition" with "haiyou"	Clause 1 ， 还有 + (,)+ Clause 2
"If…, then…" with "ruguo…, jiu…"	如果……, 就……
Expressing "every" with "mei" and "dou"	每……都……
Expressing location with "zai…shang/xia/li"	在 + Location + 上/下/里/旁边
Auxiliary verb "hui" for "will"	会 + V
"Some" using "yixie"	一些 + Noun
Expressing lateness with "cai"	才
"Yinggai" for should	应该 / 该 + V
"Always" with "zongshi"	总是 + V.
Measure words for verbs	V + Number + MW

Change of state with "le"	……了
Emphasizing quantity with "dou"	大家 / 很多人 + 都……
Verbs with "gei"	Subject + 给 + Target + Verb + Object
Emphasis with "jiu"	就 + Verb
CHAPTER 2	
"Already" with "yijing"	已经……了
Auxiliary verb "yao" and its multiple meanings	要 + Noun/要 + V
"Just now" with "gangcai"	刚才 + Verb
Expressing purpose with "weile"	为了 + Purpose + V
"Even more" with "geng"	更 + adj.
Special verbs with "hen"	很 + V
Continuation with "hai"	还 + V / Adj
Softening the tone of questions with "ne"	……呢？
Basic comparisons with "yiyang"	N1 + 跟 + N2 + 一样 + Adj
Causative verbs	N1 + 让/叫/请 + N2……
Separable verb	V-Obj / V + …… + Obj
After a specific time	Time/Time phrase + 以后
"Shi... de" construction	Subject + 是 + [information to be emphasized] + Verb + 的
Before a specific time	Time / Verb + 以前
CHAPTER 3	
"Some" with "youde"	有的 + Noun
"Just" with "gang"	Subject + 刚 + V.
"Both A and B" with "you"	又…… 又……
"Not at all"	一点(儿)也不……
Ordinal numbers with "di"	第 + Number (+ MW)
Inability with "mei banfa"	没办法 + V
"In addition" with "zaishuo"	再说……
"All along" with "yizhi"	Subject + 一直 + Predicate

Expressing "more and more" with "yue... yue..."	越⋯ 越⋯

CHAPTER 4

Expressing "all" with "shenme dou"	什么都/也
Using "ji" to mean "several"	几 + Measure Word + Noun
Mistakenly think that	以为⋯⋯
"Zai" following verbs	V + 在 + Place
Negative commands with "bie"	别 + V
Asking why with "zenme"	怎么⋯⋯?
Sentence-final interjection "a"	⋯⋯啊!

CHAPTER 5

Expressing duration (ongoing)	Verb + 了 + Duration + 了

CHAPTER 6

Difficult to do something	难 + V
Indicating a number in excess	Number + 多
"From... to..." with "cong... dao..."	从⋯⋯ 到⋯⋯

CHAPTER 7

"Ye" and "dou" together	也 + 都 + V /也 + 都 + Adj
Descriptive complements	V/Adj + 得⋯

CHAPTER 8

There are no new grammar points in this chapter.

CHAPTER 9

There are no new grammar points in this chapter.

CHAPTER 10

There are no new grammar points in this chapter.

Credits

Original Author: Sir Arthur Conan Doyle

Series Editor: John Pasden

Lead Writer: Yang Renjun

Content Editor: Yu Cui

Proofreader: Zhang Pei

Illustrator: Hu Shen

Producer: Jared Turner

Acknowledgments

We are grateful to Yang Renjun, Yu Cui, Song Shen and the entire team at AllSet Learning for working on this project and contributing the perfect mix of talent to produce this series.

Thank you to our enthusiastic testers, Ben Slye, Brandon Sanchez, Logan Pauley, Ashlyn Weber, and Ariel Bowman. Thank you to Judy Yang who helped with our cover and book design.

A special thanks to Rob Waring, to whom we refer as the "godfather of extensive reading" for his encouragement, expert advice, and support with this project.

Thank you to Heather Turner for being the inspiration behind the entire series and never wavering in her belief. Thank you to Song Shen for supporting us, handling all the small thankless tasks, and spurring us forward if we dared to fall behind.

Moreover, we will be forever grateful for Yuehua Liu and Chengzhi Chu for pioneering the first graded readers in Chinese and to whom we owe a debt of gratitude for their years of tireless work to bring these type of materials to the Chinese learning community.

About Mandarin Companion

Mandarin Companion was started by Jared Turner and John Pasden who met one fateful day on a bus in Shanghai when the only remaining seat left them sitting next to each other. A year later, Jared had greatly improved his Chinese using extensive reading but was frustrated at the lack of suitable reading materials. He approached John with the prospect of creating their own series. Having worked in Chinese education for nearly a decade, John was intrigued with the idea and thus began the Mandarin Companion series.

John majored in Japanese in college, but started learning Mandarin and later moved to China where his learning accelerated. After developing language proficiency, he was admitted into an all-Chinese masters program in applied linguistics at East China Normal University in Shanghai. Throughout his learning process, John developed an open mind to different learning styles and a tendency to challenge conventional wisdom in the field of teaching Chinese. He has since worked at ChinesePod as academic director and host, and opened his own consultancy, AllSet Learning, in Shanghai to help individuals acquire Chinese language proficiency. He lives in Shanghai with his wife and children.

After graduate school and with no Chinese language skills, Jared decided to move to China with his young family in search of career opportunities. Later while working on an investment project, Jared learned about extensive reading and decided that if it was as effective as it claimed to be, it could help him learn Chinese. In three months, he read 10 Chinese graded readers and his language ability quickly improved from speaking words and phrases to a conversational level. Jared has an MBA from Purdue University and a bachelor in Economics from the University of Utah. He lives in Shanghai with his wife and children.

Other Stories from Mandarin Companion

Level 1 Readers: 300 Characters

The Secret Garden 《秘密花园》
by Frances Hodgson Burnett

Li Ye (Mary Lennox) grew up without the love and affection of her parents. After an epidemic leaves her an orphan, Li Ye is sent off to live with her reclusive uncle in his sprawling estate in Nanjing. She learns of a secret garden where no one has set foot in ten years. Li Ye finds the garden and slowly discovers the secrets of the manor. With the help of new friends, she brings the garden back to life and learns the healing power of friendship and love.

The Monkey's Paw 《猴爪》
by W.W. Jacobs

Mr. and Mrs. Zhang live with their grown son Guisheng who works at a factory. One day an old friend of Mr. Zhang comes to visit the family after having spent years traveling in the mysterious hills of China's Yunnan Province. He tells the Zhang family of a monkey's paw that has magical powers to grant three wishes to the holder. Against his better judgement, he reluctantly gives the monkey paw to the Zhang family, along with a warning that the wishes come with a great price for trying to change ones fate…

The Sixty-Year Dream 《六十年的梦》
based on "Rip Van Winkle" by Washington Irving

Zhou Xuefa (Rip Van Winkle) is well loved by everyone in his town, everyone except his nagging wife. With his faithful dog Blackie, Zhou Xuefa spends his time playing with kids, helping neighbors, and discussing politics in the teahouse. One day after a bad scolding from his wife, he goes for a walk into the mountains and meets a mysterious old man who appears to be from an ancient time. The man invites him into his mountain home for a meal and after drinking some wine, Zhou Xuefa falls into a deep sleep. He awakes to a time very different than what he once knew.

The Country of the Blind 《盲人国》
by H.G. Wells

"In the country of the blind, the one-eyed man is king" repeats in Chen Fangyuan's mind after he finds himself trapped in a valley holding a community of people for whom a disease eliminated their vision many generations before and no longer have a concept of sight. Chen Fangyuan quickly finds that these people have developed their other senses to compensate for their lack of sight. His insistence that he can see causes the entire community to believe he is crazy. With no way out, Chen Fangyuan begins to accept his fate until one day the village doctors believe they now understand what is the cause of his insanity... those useless round objects in his eye sockets.

Mandarin companion is producing a growing library of graded readers

for Chinese language learners.

Visit our website for the newest books available:

www.MandarinCompanion.com

CPSIA information can be obtained
at www.ICGtesting.com
Printed in the USA
LVOW02s0457090716
495638LV00007B/38/P